THE SONGS OF SUMMER

Poems About Baseball

Tom Erickson and Ed Werstein, Editors

WATER'S EDGE PRESS
TUCSON, AZ

This collection of poems is a human-made work of imagination. No part of this book may be reproduced, distributed, or transmitted in any form or by any means without written permission of the publisher, except in the case of brief quotations used in a review of the book.

NO AI TRAINING: Without in any way limiting the editors' [and publisher's] exclusive rights under copyright, any use of this publication to "train" generative artificial intelligence (AI) technologies to generate text is expressly prohibited. The editors reserve all rights to license uses of this work for generative AI training and development of machine learning language models.

The Songs of Summer: Poems About Baseball
Water's Edge Press © 2025
Tom Erickson and Ed Werstein, Editors

Copyright for the collective work belongs to the publisher.
Contributors retain rights for their individual works.

ISBN: 978-1-952526-31-2

Published in the United States

Water's Edge Press LLC
Tucson, Arizona

Cover image licensed through iStock, by Getty Images
Cover and book design by Water's Edge Press

To those who have fallen in love with the rhythms of the game.

Editors' Note

We're poets and lovers of baseball. A few months ago, over a beer (and what's baseball without beer?) we discussed the fact that there had not been an anthology of baseball poems published in over ten years.

We decided to fill that gap with a new anthology. In our submission call for poems, we asked "Do you have a favorite player or team? Did you play in Little League? Did you listen to games late at night when your team was playing on the west coast? Did you play stick ball on city streets? Do you remember the first major league game you attended?"

Our goal was to assemble a collection of poems that celebrated not just the game itself, but the many ways baseball enters our lives. The poems went beyond our limited suggestions.

Here you'll find not only favorite teams and players, reminiscences about little league and pickup ball, and odes to the game, but also poems about playing catch with Dad (or Mom), getting married on a diamond, hot dogs, Cracker Jack, and yes, beer.

We hope you enjoy reading this anthology as much as we enjoyed putting it together.

                Tom Erickson and Ed Werstein

Contents

Pitchers and Catchers, Patrick Walsh 1
Spring: A Catechism, Amy Miller 2
A Night Game In Menominee Park, Susan Firer 3
Everybody is a Mets Fan Today, Margaret R. Sáraco 4
Say Hey, Paul Buchheit 7
Eamus Catuli, Mark Tardi 8
Upon Being Told, Again, that Baseball is Too Slow,
Pepper Trail 10
Town Ball, Vince Wixon 11
Baseball, Mark Hammerschick 12
Looking Out This Window Thinking of Ernie Banks
and William Carlos Williams, Kevin Miller 13
Summer Sundays, Ed Werstein 14
At the Ball Game, Tom Erickson 15
For the Love of the Game, Mario (The Poet) Willis 16
Home Plate, Sharon Daly 18
Extending Her Contract, Milton Jordan 19
Nancy Faust, Robert Chicoine 20
A Game to Remember, Jan Chronister 21
Memories of a Girl and Her Glove, Georgi Bargamian 22
Baseball Mom, Peggy Trojan 24
Minor League Baseball, Alan Harris 25
The Sound of Baseball, David Dephy 27
Roberto Clemente Catches the Last Fly Ball in Heaven,
James P. Roberts 28
At the Mazeroski Wall PNC Bank Park, Pittsburgh, PA,
Edwin Romond 31
When Asked About the Things I Wrote, I Say:,
Julián David Bañuelos 32
Poets Should Have Baseball Cards, Scott Lowery 33
Johnny Callison, Joseph Chelius 34
You're Gonna Like This Game, Dwayne Brenna 35

Bat Day at the Met, Jim Landwehr 36
Riffing On Opening Day, Sara Sarna..37
Powell, Mark Zimmermann 38
Home Team, Virginia Small..39
Second Base, Dan Kaufman..41
Centerfield Shot, Dennis Collier 42
Baseball, Ronnie Hess 43
Three Baseball Haiku, Sylvia Forges-Ryan....................................44
As the Evening Falls, Barbara Anna Gaiardoni 45
Two Haiku, Mandy Butterfield Isaacson 46
Little League Haiku, Patricia Carragon 47
108 (2016 World Series), Timothy Tocher 48
Elegy for a Dove *, Darrell Petska..49
Caught in the Web, Jack Ridl..50
Dad's AM Radio, Maggie Capettini...51
Lou Gehrig Day Yankee Stadium, July 4, 1939,
Edwin Romond...53
Against Seven-Inning Doubleheaders and Starting Runners
on Second Base in Extra Innings in Major League Baseball,
Sandra Marchetti..54
Boys and Girls of Summer, Nancy Austin 55
Summer in a Chicago Suburb not far from
the Wisconsin State Line, circa 1977, Donna Kelly...................56
Memorabilia, Scott Lowery...57
Pickup Ball, Jim Landwehr..59
On Finding a Jack Morris Baseball Card, David Jibson 61
Tigers #6, Ed Werstein 62
The Big Hurt, Tim Krcmarik 63
Boys Forever Blues, Greg Zeck..65
I Want to Be Married at Home Plate, Peter M. Gordon 67
Setting the Record Straight, Mary McKSchmidt......................68
Baseball for Girls, Jocelyn Boor 71
McGill Drive, Susan Haifleigh 72

Jimmy, Jeffrey Johannes 74
Ohtani Imayo, Bill Cushing 75
Baseball Intervenes, Tim Conlan 76
Baseball and My Dad, Joe Carey 77
Sixty-one, Bruce Dethlefsen 78
Baseball, Tom Erickson 79
Friday, 1:20, Sandra Marchetti 80
Ode to Baseball, Pepper Trail 81

THE SONGS OF SUMMER

Patrick Walsh

Pitchers and Catchers

Look, I'm not going to lie to you: I'm no big fan of winter.
At best I regard it as a kind of rest, a time for nature
To nap beneath a blanket of snow, to hibernate
Alongside her cubs and trot out shiny in spring.
But I'm no bear. I can't sleep through it and before you know,
The last bottle of champagne is upside-down in its bucket,
The party's racket — high-heel clatter, disco, and shrieks —
Won't beat out the hot water pipes creaking in woodpecker cycles:
It's the long haul, the stretch from New Year's to pitchers and catchers.

As a gesture, I grow a beard; I'll shave it off when the boys report.
I come back from a run and freeze at the mirror: there it is,
Like a Christmas tree, all trimmed in beads of frozen breath —
I've gone and dragged the enemy into the house, and me so bent
On getting him out. Sometimes I feel the winter's like a siege,
Trenches for sidewalks, a cold, concrete line of week-old snow,
And the waiting for news, that first dispatch from the South, perhaps
A short piece in the *Times*, the Yanks and Mets in exhibition.
Until then, it's a game of dead-ball, a war of attrition.

As you might have guessed, it's a whole lot more than baseball —
The game just takes me back, aside from any innocence of its own,
To when I was younger, when life set so many diamonds before me
And I stood before life error-free. Now, each winter brings it home:
I'm still waiting for my pitchers and catchers to report. I've minored
In everything — you should read my résumé. So many strong starts
I've ditched on account of pride, disillusionment. Anyway,
It's never been about a career but life, mine matchless
With love and daily joy. The neighbors dig out; I dig in.

Amy Miller

Spring: A Catechism

Baseball takes
as long as it takes.
An inning is like
reciprocal dinners: first
they eat, then we do.
The shortstop's throw
is a hairpin shape:
leg and arm
snap, a bow
of brittle energy.
A cloud pulls
shadows across the field.

We're all small,
sturdy animals stunned
by the April sun, wedged
hip on hip, peanut shells
all over our shoes. We watch
the men out there. We speak
their Spanish,
their Irish names,
speak their same
strange language:
Split-finger. Short porch.
Wheelhouse. Fly.

Susan Firer

A Night Game In Menominee Park

A night game in Menominee Park,
where the ladies hit the large white balls
like stars through the night they roll
like angel food cake batter folded through devil's food.
Again, I want to hear the fans' empty beer cans
being crushed—new ones hissing open.
"You're a gun, Anna"
"She can't hit"
"Lay it on."
Oh, run, swift softball women
under the lights the Kiwanis put in.
Be the wonderful sliding night
animals I remember. Remind me constantly
of human error and redemption.
Hit
ball after ball to the lip of the field
while the lake flies fall like confetti
under the park's night lights.
Sunlight Dairy Team, remember me
as you lift your bats,
pump energy into
them bats, whirling circular as helicopter
blades above your heads.
Was it the ball Julie on the Honey-B-Tavern team
hit toward my head that made me so soft-
ball crazy that right in the middle of a tune
by Gentleman Jim's Orchestra, here in Bingo-Polka
Heaven at Saint Mary of Czestochowa's annual Kielbasa
Festival, I go homesick for Oshkosh women's softball?
I order another another Kielbasa and wonder
If Donna will stay on third next game or
again run head down wild into Menominee home plate.
Play louder, Gentleman Jim.
Saint Mary of Czestochowa throws a swell festival, but
Oshkosh women's softball—that's a whole other ballgame.

Margaret R. Sáraco

Everybody is a Mets Fan Today

October 15, 1986

Mets lead the Astros 3 games to 2 in the playoffs.
Game 6, they score 3 in the ninth. Extra innings?
Got to catch the subway to the city to go to work.
Can't carry the 13-inch TV.
Don't own a portable radio.

Race down Washington.
Jump on and off the PATH
Arrive at Christopher.
Scale stairs two-at-a-time.
Jaywalk between speeding taxis.

Interred underground for how many innings?

Dash to the acting studio at Fourth and First.
Will anyone have a radio or (fingers crossed) small tv?
Personal detection system alerted—
people cluster around a window cheering.

They have the game on.

45,718 people at the Astrodome and we huddle
on the sidewalk peer into a ground-floor apartment.
Bottom of the twelfth, Mets in the field.

Roger McDowell on the mound.
Two out, Kevin Bass on first.
Batter up!
Sixteen-year veteran Jose Cruz at the plate.
Bass is a stealer and crazy fast. Two strikes on Cruz.
Gary Carter throws out Bass at second from home!
"Come on McDowell, sit 'em down!" I yell.
Bouncing ball and he's thrown out!

Margaret R. Sáraco

Cheering. Jumping.
"Gotta go," as the Astros take the field.
Sprint to the next window.
The game's not over.
Sprint to the next window.
Adrenaline pumping. "Gotta go!"
Fist bumps all around.
Bleeding orange and blue
throw open the theater doors.

It is damn quiet.

Really? No one has the game on?
Come on. What is it about theater people?
Find a transistor in the desk drawer.
Tune to 1050 WHN, static, volume to 10.
Actors mill in the hallway waiting for classes.
Ask questions. I put my finger to my lips.
Listen. Crack of the bat. Wait! Another hit?

The Astros enter the bottom of the sixteenth,
trailing by 3, the score 7-4.
Bullpens depleted.
Jesse Orosco on the mound since the fifteenth
running on empty.
No one wants to face Astros Ace Mike Scott
and his lethal splitter for Game 7.

Oh, no! Oh, no! Orosco gives up a run.
And another!
7-6 everything on the line.

Lock the office door.
Can't be bothered with stupid questions.

Margaret R. Sáraco

Should have called in sick.
Sure as hell feeling sick now.

Wait! Wait! What?

After 4 hours and 42 minutes,
travelling from Hoboken to the East Village,
window to window, and to work…

The Mets Win the Ball Game!
The Mets Win the Ball Game!
They're in the World Series!

Put it in the books!

Paul Buchheit

Say Hey

The Catch! A fan will think of Willie Mays,
the Polo Grounds in Nineteen-Fifty-Four,
his back to home — of all the greatest plays,
it's Number One. But there's forevermore
a play that almost made the Giant yield
his title. Softball slugger Roundy Horn
was batting, smashed a ball to center field,
the deepest part — the Polo Grounds reborn!
Our super shortstop, Mikey Casey, passed
the center fielder…ball was near the fence…
with perfect timing, racing back as fast
as superstars can run…for all intents
and purposes a homer…at the wall
he leaped!…but Mikey Casey dropped the ball.

Mark Tardi

Eamus Catuli

"Chicago is an October sort of city even in spring." –Nelson Algren

Because a decade doubled with grace

Because, yes, there are entirely too many strikeouts
& only one Tony Gwynn

some outcomes as likely
as finding platypi

in Virginia tomato fields

the carved silence of
a perfect bunt

its own kind of song

the spit seeds & covenants, nicely aisled
for a public daydream

on repeat

a century of expectations flung
like Sandberg to Dunston
to Addison

or lake trout to penguin

Because if the spirit sanctifies it, every
scorecard becomes a bible

bartered with ifs
& almosts & painted corners

Mark Tardi

Because I was born 99 years after Mordecai Brown

with all my fingers
but that foul ball
is still just out of reach

Upon Being Told, Again, that Baseball is Too Slow

for Vince Wixon

No, I would say that it is not slow enough
I would wish it to be slower, in slow motion
So that a game would consume, not a lazy summer afternoon
But an entire day, from cock-crow to moon-rise

Then, inside those elongated moments
It might be possible at last to see as they see
The bright lines between cutter and slider and slurve
The spin rate on that tumbling meteor, the fastball

To devote the time that it deserves
To the pitcher's finger-magic before the throw
To the instant that the third baseman's feet leave Earth
To the ballistics of line drive striking pocket of mitt

But even then we would never know, we mortals
How the batter meditates as windup leads to pitch
How the fielder begins to move before the crack of bat
The choreography of double play across ninety feet of roar

Yes, I can appreciate the headlong pace of hoops
And for those who require violence, football's brutal draw
But those are only games to me, while baseball, baseball
Baseball stops time, when nothing else will

Vincent Wixon

Town Ball

High school and college summers center field was my domain,
playing alongside men in their thirties and forties who farmed,
ran the elevator, sold seed corn, worked construction.
They focused on swinging for the fences, not running down fly balls
on sticky August Southwest Minnesota Sunday afternoons
in wool uniforms with "Engineers" stitched on the front.
"Anything you can get to, Willie," they called from left and right.

Engineers because, in its salad days, Tracy was a railroad center.
Laura Ingalls Wilder waited in the depot for the train to South Dakota.
You could look it up. Those days were long gone, the depot gone,
roundhouse, too, and the two hotels where railroad men put up,
those who wore striped bib overalls and caps and played cards
and drank 3.2 beer in my uncle's pool hall.

One night, before my time, a few players got drunk after a game
and commandeered an engine down the line as far as Garvin
before coming to their senses. How many times
after games had I heard that story in bars where Merle,
the town's best player ever, bought me 10-High Sours.

Carp, Big Daddy, Sam, Curt, Pus Arm, Hoss, Billy, Flame Thrower,
Bo, Lefty, Flatty, Harmbogy—I played with them, then it was over:
my education in dugouts and in cars riding to unkempt ballparks
with smart, funny, vulgar men who returned to work on Monday,
and I left soon after for another kind of learning.

Mark Hammerschick

Baseball

like the history it came from
as the boys came back
from a civil war
it galvanized a moment in time
when the focus of a world
went from annihilation to unity
to sliders curveballs fastballs
on emerald carpets
like the ivy at Wrigley Field
a Green Monster at Fenway
and the hallowed ground at Yankee Stadium
where giants played the game
Ruth, Gehrig, Mantle, DiMaggio.
Time has no limits in the ballpark.
This is not Football.
This is not Basketball.
This is not Hockey.
This is not Soccer.
There is no clock.
The game takes as long as it needs to
until one team wins.
Like a nation forged in the pursuit
of life, liberty and the pursuit of happiness
this game echoes
the grit of our Republic
this game is our childhood
it's how we learn to be human
scoring, striking out, winning and losing.
And in that knowing
we watch that lean slow curve
as it comes in
and we swing.

Kevin Miller

**Looking Out This Window Thinking
of Ernie Banks and William Carlos Williams**

The broken handled wheelbarrow leans
into its third spring, propped like
a knothole kid against the side fence.

The games go on, those of us benched
because of age understand quiet is
like a rainout, we pause to rebuild tired

arms, recover from losses, slumps, errors.
We have time to turn this thing around, rally.
The rookies are immortal, they laugh

and tip their caps from the end of the bench
understanding parts ritual and superstition.
We never pack the bats till the last out.

Ed Werstein

Summer Sundays

Out the back door
at the homestead,
came our fathers and uncles,
lumbering down the gentle slope
posturing, boasting,
warning us to get ready.

Not so much tired of their card game
as chased by Grandma and our aunts
who needed the table
to prepare our dinner.

They folded their spades and hearts
and invaded our diamond,
raised our clubs, our bats, our lumber,
their strong limbs with enough left
after a long week of factory and farm
to teach us a thing or two about baseball.

Tom Erickson

At the Ball Game

We stopped to buy a scorecard at the gift shop.
We missed buying it from the vendor who used
to have a stand right where we walked into the stadium
but the stand was gone. We missed how it used to be
when the pitcher hit and when there were more
Black players and when there were double switches
so the extra line on the scorecard was a gift.

We didn't really miss the metal bleachers
that were cold in April or the snazzy cars
that used to drive the relief pitchers from the bullpen
to the mound and how we felt embarrassed
for the pitcher and the driver. We have to admit
that we like the pitch clock but we don't want to.
We don't know what to think about the walk-up music—
a lot of songs in Spanish for the Latino players
and country songs for the white guys. We wonder
what Willie Mays would have been listening to
when he walked up to the plate. We think Sam Cooke
or maybe Ella Fitzgerald. We kind of like all the new
stats even though we already knew that "a walk
is as good as a hit" at least if that hit was a single
back when we were playing Little League. We ponder
if a pitcher would rather have a quality start or a win—
either pitch six innings and give up three runs and lose
or pitch five innings and give up four runs and win.
We agree the answer is obvious but still…

We kind of don't like that it's $12 for a beer
but it's a full count and a dollar says
the next pitch is a foul ball.
And the innings fly by.

Mario (the Poet) Willis

For the Love of the Game

the infield littered with sweat
cleats packed with sand & blood
the love of the game pours out
in the roar of the crowd
Giants, Monarchs, Grays, Clowns, and Bears
the round ball turns bending in the air
like a clock's hand set on a time
when men were separated
by color of skin
the jersey & caps were an afterthought
Satchel Page, Octavious Cotto, Nip Winters, Josh Gibson
the ropes to hold back the crowds
to watch men play a kid's game
bent elbow & the crack of the bat
couldn't tell you what color the man who struck it was
as it rushed over the fence into the sea of faces
cheering for their heroes

barnstorming from town to town
long before Jackie Robinson's star had been lifted
into the Brooklyn sky
Cap Anson would have rolled in his grave
a gentleman's agreement broken
Commissioner Landis would have spit and screamed
to watch Doby & Satchel Paige
brothers taking Championship glory
back to their Negro homes
the game still groans
to think it was ever used to separate men
when these diamonds and green grass
were intended to bring us together
to cheer the accomplishment of American Legends
batting, curving. and sliding into our hearts
with the memories of magic summers.

Mario (the Poet) Willis

the days of the Cuban Giants behind us
the glory of the Chicago Union a distant memory
long after Rube Foster built an institution
years since Greenlee's East West Classic
well after Effa Manley calls for solidarity
the names of the Negro legends are cemented in Cooperstown
Cyclone Joe, Turkey Stearnes, the Devil Wells
the heart swells with the pride of stars made immortal

the game may never again know Jim Crow's filthy eyes
may never require men to lie about their heritage again to play it
the chills of the Anthem's glory are for all it's sons
this our American game for all his sons
under the open air & sunlight they play
catch, and steal
till our memories are star spangled like the flag
the foul poles remember
our less venerable times
and how far the ball would travel when
Hammerin' Hank draped in a Clowns Jersey
would round the bases
A full blown legend in both the White & Negro Leagues
if only we would take time to remember.

Sharon Daly

Home Plate

On summer Saturdays, I straddled the frayed nylon
straps of the lounge chair on the borderland between
the New York Yankees and the Pittsburgh Pirates.
Each swing of the bat provoked as much pain and pleasure
as the pungent Limburger cheese my father spread thick
on dark rye with raw onions that made me weep.
The portable antenna was tuned to the announcer
calling balls and strikes and lauding the legendary
Bill Mazeroski, aka "The Glove"
and Roberto Clemente, "the right field wonder."
My dad held the plate, offering bites that expanded
the taste of childhood beyond our rickety porch to Forbes Field,
filled with cheering fans and sunlit grass of well-tended beauty,
so unlike the weed-choked lawn that surrounded us.
We always hoped the score would go our way,
imagined the soles of the players we rooted for rounding
the bases, the sharp tang of Limburger and onions
suffused in the air, finding their way home.

Milton Jordan

Extending Her Contract

The Botanist on a Visiting Assistant
Professor contract who shared our small
Science Center office held a particular
interest in the regional grasses
covering our campus along a minor
tributary feeding the lower Brazos
and we asked her to focus that interest
on the thin grass cover of our infield.

What you have here, she said, *is a hopeless case.*
Without a total recomposition
this alkaline soil cannot support
the Coastal Bermuda you're using,
Johnson Grass will take over in bunches
and the transfer portal claim your best infielders.

She could not, though, resist the challenge,
and brought us, a week later, soil formulas,
contractors' estimates with projected
schedules and her contract extension request.

Work began under her supervision
in early January and the Pirate
Nine played that season on a ragged
city park field with loud visitor complaints.

A year later, after fall ball in the park
and February on the road, we started March
with a smiling shortstop fielding a clean
ground ball off her well-manicured green infield,
an inning ending double play, our Botanist
exclaiming, This is a beautiful game!

Robert Chicoine

Nancy Faust

(Faust was the White Sox organist from 1970 through 2010, and again in 2025)

This steady shower, like the game, shall not be timed.
Here we are in the middle of the rain
in the middle of the game
in mid-evening in the middle
of our lives. And our organist,
whose time this is, is in the middle
of yet another tune after a segue so deft
we didn't notice it. She has played these rains
since we were young, old love;
there is no end to her repertoire.
Her ear, unerring, can flesh out
anything we can hum from your two notes
and my one. Now, per requests
from the sibilance in the air and the drumbeat
on the infield tarp, she is playing
to the downpours in Beethoven's *Pastoral Symphony*
and Vivaldi's presto *Summer*.
Next she'll break into Credence Clearwater Revival.
But we are too rippled, too tranquil;
you and I are not the ones to stop the rain.

Oh, in time the game will resume.
This is no night for defeat or victory!
Only for outcomes, eventually.
Don't you worry about a thing --
unless Nancy begins playing
"Nearer My God to Thee"

Jan Chronister

A Game to Remember

Hank Aaron, Eddie Mathews, Lou Burdette.
At eight years old I knew their stats the way
kids today know characters on a screen.
I listened to games on my tiny transistor
under a sheet tent late at night.

Next day I'd check the stats
in the Milwaukee Journal—
batting average, RBIs, ERA.
I understood what they meant
but not the math involved.
I bought Bazooka bubble gum,
had a shoebox full of cards

In '57 my dad took me to a game—
just me, no brother or sister.
I think he needed a day off
from pressures at work,
worries at home, someplace
he could let off steam.
He got his chance when Burdette
pitched his 500th strikeout.

That was the only year
the Braves won the World Series.
That was the only day
my dad spent time with me alone.

Georgi Bargamian

Memories of a Girl and Her Glove

You're on your side of the street,
And I'm on mine,
Punching my fist into
The palm of my glove
For a game of catch.

You throw first and I catch the ball,
With the satisfying sting that
Feels like purpose,
Feels like winning.
I draw my arm back and pitch back to you.

We're at Fenway Park with
Carl Yastrzemski and Rico Petrocelli and Tony C.
You tell me your next pitch is a high pop and
I step back, glove in the air,
Hoping it drops into the pocket,
Not wanting to disappoint you
Or our pretend teammates.

The hot summer sun
And cars that pass
Don't dampen our spirit
Or drown out the crowd
That cheers us on
For the faith in our promise,
The depth of our hopes,
The sweep of our dreams.

You're still in New England
Rooting for the Sox
And I'm in Michigan
Rooting for the Tigers wondering

Georgi Bargamian

Whether you think the game
Feels as immense as it did
When I was on my side of street
And you were on yours
Holding a baseball in your hand
In the lightness of youth.

Peggy Trojan

Baseball Mom

for Laura

I came to your games,
Little League to high school varsity.
Froze wearing sleeping bags,
shivered in pouring rain.
Sat on steel bleachers in blazing sun
through extra innings, thinking
I should be making supper.
Drove to out-of-town games,
kept my tongue
when rude fans yelled advice,
screaming just how
you could have made that run.
Knew all the players,
my screechy cheering ready,
my hands clapped red
for winning hits.
One would assume
I am a serious baseball fan.
I did not spend all those
afternoons for baseball.
I came to watch you.

Alan Harris

Minor League Baseball

Fridays
7:05 game time
seated down the third base line
the setting sun at my back
a bag of peanuts in my lap
my old Wilson rawhide at my side, just in case
to cheer on my Lansing Lugnuts
as they chase down line drives and big league dreams

Tickets are cheap. Beer is cold. Hot dogs are perfect.

I can do without the rain.
And if it's less than 45 degrees or more than 92, forgive me if I stay at home. There will always be another game.

I can also do without
professional autograph hounds
Should be an age limit to hang out by the dugout
to get a ball player's signature on a future investment.
I'd be okay if that age limit was 9 ½ years old.
Please get out of line if you're older than the kid in the uniform
whose signature you are stealing.

Children don't steal signatures. They cherish them.

I love The Curly Shuffle and the t-shirt toss.
I'm a big fan of Big Lug.
I'm reminded during the seventh inning-stretch
that of the two songs I have completely memorized,
Take Me Out to the Ball Game is one of them.

And when the game is over on a Friday night,
I remain seated, awaiting the wonder of fireworks.
Sparks of magic. Baseball magic. A day worth remembering.

Alan Harris

There will always be another game—until there isn't.

I hope you come out next Friday.
I hope you find me seated along the third base line
with the setting sun at my back
a bag of peanuts in my lap
my old Wilson mitt by my side; you know, just in case.

David Dephy

The Sound of Baseball

I watched the Yankees game for the very first time
in my life at the Yankee Stadium in the Bronx,
sitting in a premium seat. Boy, how lucky I am.

The Yankees played the Seattle Mariners
and won 5-0. As a New Yorker, I was like, "Let's go,
Yankees, let's go!" Man, it was my first Yankees game—

a touch of a miracle. A massive impression of otherworldly
experience, totally unforgettable, an explosively powerful
spirit of freedom, or even revelation that stays with you for life.

I always thought that something indescribable and almighty
dwelt in the heart of baseball, but the Yankees and Mariners
showed me not only that heart, but the divinity of the United

States of America, home. And now, feeling the rolling waves
of a frisbee underneath the sounds of baseball and laughter,
memories are shivering in my thoughts. They are not bridges

to the past, but in the future, that's how the prophecy works.
If they are deep enough, they will reach the future far enough.
We are all children of changes. Changes are not linear; only

when looking back, do the turns make sense, stepping on the
fields, walking on the rays at dawn, feeling the pulsation of the
earth under your feet, nothing will change you— everything

reveals you, and one day, looking back, you won't find what
you've left behind that familiar feeling of the rolling waves
of a frisbee, baseball, and laughter remains the same.

James P. Roberts

Roberto Clemente Catches the Last Fly Ball in Heaven

He does not know how it happened,
but he is back, here in right field,
standing, half-bent over, hands on knees

watching the Pirate pitcher go into his windup.
He recognizes the game, the situation.
It is the fifth inning of the seventh game

of the 1971 World Series. Boog Powell, the massive
Baltimore Oriole first baseman is at the plate, waving
that menacing bat back and forth, waiting for his pitch.

Ellis—or is it Blass?—leans in. The figure on the mound
shimmers in the heat of the afternoon in this, the final
World Series to be played entirely in the daytime.

Everything goes blurry, but even before he hears the crack
of the bat, his legs are pistoning back
and to his right, his eyes now picking up the ball

streaking for the gap between himself and Clines—
or is it Jeter?—in center. The runners on first
and second are on the move, but he feels that he

has a chance. But then the scene suddenly shifts.
It is September 28, 1972, the final game of the season
against the Mets. Jon Matlack is on the mound, his young

face studious, sheened with sweat. Matlack's pitch
floats in and your 38-year-old body still has the reflexes
to time it, pivot the aching hip, snap of the wrist

James P. Roberts

and the ball is lined out into right-center field
for hit number 3,000. It is done, the ball is returned
to you, standing on second base and you softly toss it

toward the Pirate bat boy, who has come out to take care
of what will end up on your mantle at home in Puerto Rico,
along with your other awards and trophies. The crowd,

as it has so often before, rises to its feet, clapping
for their hero. All the rancor and discord of the past, forgotten,
absolved. Clemente! Clemente! Clemente!

Again, a blur and you are now in a different place. It is small
and crowded with boxes and crates of relief supplies,
tied down beneath a tarpaulin as the plane takes off,

heading for Nicaragua. Your face is lined with worry,
you are afraid of what may be waiting at the other end.
Danger amidst a disaster, but you are resolved to help.

A jolt, a whirling spin and something is dreadfully wrong.
You find yourself trapped beneath the broken cargo,
the plane sinks in rising waters. You can't . . .

But Manny is there, old number 35, reaching out his hand
and you feel the strong brown grip. A white light shines
briefly—and there is the ball, descending just over

your head. You stick up your glove, leaving your feet,
and feel the sharp tug as the ball strikes and the glove
closes. The ground feels soft as a pillow, or a cloud.

James P. Roberts

The Pirates win the World Series; you hit three home runs,
throw out runners left and right, saying to the world:
This is who I am. But not who you will become?

An indelible image: 21 and 35 running off the field
together, headed toward that final destiny. In his dreams,
Manny Sanguillen is still diving cold waters, searching.

Edwin Romond

At the Mazeroski Wall PNC Bank Park, Pittsburgh, PA

for John Cosgrove

It gives me the creeps, this red brick wall
with its faded 406. I could have my picture
taken in front of it but, for a Yankee fan,
it'd be tasteless as posing with a tomb stone.

The plaque says, October 13, 1960, the day I ran
all the way home from 6th grade for the last minutes
of the 7th game of the Yankees-Pirates World Series.
I kept yelling, "Come on! Come on!" at our old TV,

begging it to warm up till finally Ralph Terry
emerged in black and white, getting the sign,
winding up and hurling his fastball to
Bill Mazeroski, who smacked it out to left field.

Yogi looked as if he would catch it, but then
it sailed over his head, over the wall that stands
right in front of me 50 years later. How crushing
at age 11 to lose the World Series and

part of my heart aches to see that wall up close
and remember Yogi in front of it helpless
as that little squirt Mazeroski danced around
the bases and Pittsburgh started to party

like pirates with rum and trunks of stolen gold.

Julián David Bañuelos

When Asked About the Things I Wrote, I Say:

```
the move.
90 feet            one place to the other
my mother                walking our belongings
in the dead of night          where cicadas roared
our nightly dance             devouring the dark
every night             for what seemed like the whole summer.
And I remember              one night in particular
I had reached           that portion of my closet
dusty corners           where we send things to die
and in the corner           a box filled with cowhide
cork and yarn.          And between the alleyways of seams
signatures              practiced and practiced
in other gaps           loves poems
meant to knock          someone off their feet
and out the park.        A poem is a frozen rope
(Insert moon shot).     This one to Roxanne
this one                to Mercedes this one to Alexi
each one a strikeout    turned reminder
the hit and runs              on a young heart.
The next day            I carried those poems close
walked them down            the street to the backstop
next to the church          our summer home.
I forced a few between           the chain links
the others              I tossed into the air
and smacked             into the tall fescue.
I left parts of me      that day, that summer
was the summer we            never stopped dreaming.
```

Scott Lowery

Poets Should Have Baseball Cards

with their bios charted on the flip side: major
prizes, big-league debut and teaching gigs
followed, for the well-known few, by a string
of gradually stranger titles, lists that could pinch-hit
as poems themselves. No bubble-gum—instead,
each with a fresh whiff of personal penchant:
French Roast, good weed, an earthy single malt.

But a new one with each next book. I'd trade you
my complete Gary Snyders for Stafford's rookie card—
look how young, both of them! Some author photos
inexplicably unchanging, Marianne Moore forever
in her black tri-corner hat. Neighborhood kids
would square off in sidewalk fantasy slams:
New Formalists versus Beats in the World Series.

Like baseball cards, they'd show up at garage sales,
or maybe marking a page in an old cookbook.
Unlike baseball cards, their value would increase
when dog-eared, beer-stained—strangely indestructible.

Driving on third-tier commercial streets, you'd notice
small pop-up storefronts: Poet Cards Bought & Sold.
Some nights, a small crowd inside with battered
three-ring binders, conjuring matchups, closed eyes reverent,
declaiming by heart. If you had two clothespins,
you could clamp the cards against your bike spokes,
letting loose their clackety, free-swinging song
like a whole flock of sparrows or grounders or
hometown poets, filling your ears, the best game in town.

Joseph Chelius

Johnny Callison

Little Americans' Bus Trip to Connie Mack Stadium, Late 1960s

In the right field bleachers at Connie Mack,
the Little Americans are calling out
to their favorite player as he trots on the field, puzzled
when he won't look up—won't smile or wave.
At eight and nine they are too young to imagine
that a star from a town as modest
as Qualls, Oklahoma, might shy from attention
as from a high and tight pitch.
Or brood over his last at-bat,
wondering all the while about his diminishing power—
home run totals like plummeting degrees.
Better as they sit like recruits in their LA caps
to occupy themselves with the sights around them—
the pristine field, the Ballantine sign,
the vendors with their silver carts.
Better to wait for the teams to change sides
so they can shout *Hey, Henry!*
to the Braves' Hank Aaron, who slips them
an obliging wave before the inning gets underway
and he settles into position—
hands on knees, as their coaches taught.

You're Gonna Like This Game

Pick-up truck brush-painted red
careening through the silent clouds of dust.
My dad is in the driver's seat,
skinny, way too young to be a dad,
wheat chaff on the shoulders of his shirt.
He guns it up the hill;
my stomach's in my throat.
Weeee-hooooooooo!
I'm sitting right beside him
staring at a baseball glove,
my brother's pancake hand-me-down.
Nicely broken in, my dad would say.
I've got my fingers crossed,
hoping I'll be good.

Then we're on the blacktop;
Wooden posts go speeding by.
My dad says, *Think you're gonna like this game?*
I tell him yeah but I'm not sure.
We purr through town,
End up near the school,
A dozen kids already there,
swinging bats at blue belly flies.
The red door creaking open.
Don't forget your cap!
And just before it shuts
I hear my dad
Don't be shy, he says, *and tell 'em you can pitch.*

Jim Landwehr

Bat Day at the Met

Metropolitan Stadium, 1973

Our one day at the ballpark every summer
was courtesy of our grandma
to say she was a baseball fanatic
only serves to cheapen the adjective

On Bat Day one year she took three of us
seated in the upper grandstand
thirty-seven stories above a field of green
bases looked like Chiclets

By the third inning boredom set in
when our attention turned concessionary
because while we liked baseball
a boy's stomach only has two good innings

Thirty-seven stories up, it's a different game
pop flies look bound for the stars
a ball looks like a strike and vice versa
but the ice cream vendor stands tall

Five innings into a pitching duel
thousands of other bored kids
pounded their souvenir bats on the risers
creating juvenile thunder for the home team

I remember grandma scored the games
writing Mandarin symbols in the program
a shorthand account of Bat Day history
penned so she could see what she missed

Riffing On Opening Day

The guy fresh up from the minors
hits a home run.
The veteran strikes out looking.
These days fielders wear an earpiece
and talk to commentators

while fielding.

There are fewer drunks
because of the price of beer,
fewer families because
of the price of hot dogs.

We forgot how green
grass can be,
how bright the sun,
how our hearts collectively
break or burst
with each swing of the bat.

Don't we all want
a hard plastic seat
and a slow foul ball
on Opening Day?

Powell

I saw the best Boog of any generation destroy the ball, hammering
hysterical taters—going
going… gone! over the fence into angry Yankee Mudville streets, Boog
who clipped the hippest Angel pitchers' wings, torquing imported
fastballs by Louisville connection
    c-r-r-rack, rawhide hissing into waves of trans-continental night,
Boog
who dreamed of hot dogs in the dugout,
who sent hollow-eyed hurlers to cold water showers
    —moonshots floating across the tops of cities—soon
    contemplating Boog from the minor leagues, Boog
who psyched out hurlers in enemy bullpens and saw unshaven stunned
    closers staggering on mounds illuminated, seraphim who blew
  the three-run lead with sweaty eyeballs hallucinating Boog's grand slam
    and insane tragedy of waivers; who got tossed by the ump
for ranting and crazy obscene gestures while Boog trotted around first,
who cowered naked in locker-rooms, no women allowed, burning Boog
baseball cards in wastebaskets, chewing that awful Topps gum,
    listening to The Big Game through roaring coliseum walls
    of AM transistor radio, who got their pubic bells rung
    in bush league Laredo by screaming line drives Boog hit all the way
from Baltimore, brain-throbbing agony beneath the codpiece of the
skull,
who dreamed of chin music in Greyhound buses, who vanished in
Poughkeepsie or Peoria with purgatoried dreams, nightmare
  of bobble-head Oriole doll, spitball and Amerika and endless Boog…

Home Team

We created a diamond
in the space
between the barn, the shed
and the garage.

Coaching even preschoolers,
Daddy taught eight girls and four boys
how to stand just so over the plate,
how to pitch the ball
to keep it from being hit,
how to "run like the dickens"
and use a glove like a net,
how to score a clinch run
with a daredevil bunt.

Gray-haired, he confided once or twice
that he and Uncle George
might have tried for the Big Time
if it hadn't been for the farm.

Summer evenings, after frenzied supper cleanup,
all of us kids eventually got our turn
at bat, elbows outstretched,
showing off our form
and winning his pat on the back.
Even the little kids sometimes belted
a mean line drive
or leaped to snare a pop-up.

We bickered over wearing the best gloves
and whether base runners were safe
and we cheered great plays
on either side.

Virginia Small

As twilight threatened
to cut short our family game
we stood at attention
in the batter's zone,
on the bases,
in the outfield—
my father's shadow everywhere,
everywhere.

Dan Kaufman

Second Base

With double plays, the pivot's key.
Look the ball into your glove,
then feed a belt-high flip to your shortstop
for the relay. Or if it's you
straddling second, grab the toss,
turn and peg a strike to first—all this
as you evade a runner bent on wreckage.

At a youth baseball camp, Jim Gilliam,
the 60's Dodgers' second sacker, told us:
Steady eyes and shifty feet. No two chances are the same.

There've been 240 fathers and sons
who've played Major League baseball.
My dad and I were not among them.
His back a temperamental 41 when I was born,
we rarely played catch.

In '63, we lived near the Gilliams
and Saturdays I'd shoot driveway hoops
with his son, who often wore a Lakers shirt
with Elgin Baylor's 22.
I asked him, *Don't you wanna be a Dodger?*
He pivoted, blew by me for a layup.
Won't never be my dad, he said.

Centerfield Shot

The centerfield camera in any park
shows a pair of older gents
in the front row, left of home,
conversing. Quite the vantage:
the catcher motioning fielders
into position, crouching before
the umpire. The runner at second
scrutinizing signs being flashed
by the backstop, ignoring the feints
of the shortstop when the pitcher
moves into his stretch, ascertains
the distance between runner and base,
the likelihood of steal, or pickoff.
The arc of the ball before it bends
toward the catcher, invisible as
it crosses the plate. Called to
awareness by the crack of leather
on wood, the men observe the rising
ball, the runner trotting toward third
evaluating the outcome,
fielders moving to catch the fly,
cover a base, back up a throw.

Once each game, in a later inning,
a batter fouls a pitch straight back
that slaps the screen in front
of the old men, so startled you expect
one to keel over. But they laugh,
shake it off, continue to converse.

Ronnie Hess

Baseball

I can still
smell the mitt's
oils, feel the leather,
the warm fit
of my hand
in its glove,
pitcher's
or first baseman's,
I didn't know, care.
I was a Dodgers fan,
Gil Hodges my favorite,
his quiet grace.

The Dodgers played
in Brooklyn, so far
my father took me
to see another league
at Yankee Stadium, a handful
of subway stops from home.

Dressed up, going to a game
with Daddy, wearing
my dark green
sweater set.

Sylvia Forges-Ryan

Three Baseball Haiku

Waiting to bat
the hitter swats
a swarm of gnats

Sandlot players
a mockingbird sings
the umpire's call

Rained out
the coos of pigeons echo
in the empty stadium

Barbara Anna Gaiardoni

As the Evening Falls

as the evening falls
boys gather to play baseball
in the neighborhood

Mandi Butterfield Isaacson

Two Haiku

April 17th

Ty Cobb, Tyrannosaurus
Rex, with sharpened cleats
bloodied basemen's legs

Catch Phrase

If you want a pick me up
read Yogi Berra's quotes
They never get old!

Little League Haiku

his glove reaches for the ball
falls short of his dad's
expectations

sitting out the game
with a sore arm
a kid's dream strikes out

foul ball
breaking wind
in the grandstand

fastball
to home plate . . .
you're out!

out at third
he can't outrun
a speeding ball

full count
bases loaded
all eyes on the pitcher

crack of the bat
she bunts
to first

sliding into home plate
the seam on her shorts
gives way

Timothy Tocher

108 (2016 World Series)

One hundred eight stitches on a baseball—
One for each year since the Cubs last won the title.
Each season a wound,
Each stitch a suture.
Victory at last!
The gash heals without a scar.
One hundred eight days till pitchers and catchers.

Darrell Petska

Elegy for a Dove *

> *"I just go where I'm told and do what I was made to do,"*
> *from Lisa Carver's song, "Bullet"*

I harbored no ill will toward that bird:
where the Big Unit threw, I went!

At 100 miles per, the world is a blur—
a half-second to the pop of the glove

or the "poof" of a dove-in-passing
as I bulleted toward home plate.

The flurry of feathers haunts me still:
weren't we just navigating air,

fast and free as we were made to be?
There were no winners that day

except for YouTube, replaying
that horror several million times since.

Would I have been a strike, ball, wild pitch?
Moot distinction, fate having intervened:

the ump ruled "no pitch." Statistically
I never happened. Explain that to the bird.

> ** On March 24, 2001, during a spring training game, Arizona Diamondbacks pitcher Randy Johnson accidentally hit and killed a flying dove with a fastball.*

Jack Ridl

Caught in the Web

It's been written and written about—father
and son playing catch. Toss. Catch. Throw

hard. Catch in the web. Toss. Reach for
and catch a high hard one. Catch in the

web. We're in the backyard, my father
and I playing catch, the only time and

the only way we talked to one another. Every
important decision in the remainder of my life

flew there between us, carried by the ball, its
stitches twirling indefinitely toward me, my

glove, the web. Each of his throws held a comma,
a question mark, at times an exclamation point.

There I learned that only if the arm's release
was luckily precise could there be a period at

the end of his ambiguous demands. He never said
a word about politics, the future, sex, belief in God.

The answer was in the way he threw, the way I caught.

Maggie Capettini

Dad's AM Radio

it was a rectangular box
with a couple of knobs –

the tuner could slide across
a narrow window of numbers
but it never did: always tuned
to 720. silver and black,
the size of half a cereal box
with a boxy handle and dangerous
antenna that stabbed upward
from our scuffed garage floor

where Dad would listen
nonstop and top-volume on
weekends as he worked
on this or that, tuned in to every

Cubs game: Harry + Steve's stories and
statistical didacticisms filling time
between plays, fervor entering their timbres
as the game picked up pace – the crack of the bat,
the pulse of the crowd, and Dad root,
root, rooting out loud for those loveable
Cubbies…this was the soundtrack of
summers in my grade-school days,

before HD anything – even though
a tall tower pumped the Voice of Chicago
with 50,000 watts of broadcasting power
from fractionary-miles high corporate
churches of glass and steel,
to steelyards, to corn cribs,
to rolling rural hills,

Maggie Capettini

it still sounded as though
they were inside a tin can,
talking to us through a child's play
telephone of empty soup and a string –

somehow synchronously
distant
and intimate.

Edwin Romond

Lou Gehrig Day Yankee Stadium, July 4, 1939

for BJ Ward

He was scared and did not
want to speak to 62,000 people.

Maybe he felt facing death
was enough to endure but

they kept calling his name
till he stepped up to the mic

and gave 278 words of thank you
and goodbye. His body trembled

as he spoke with the voice
of a dying man still strong enough

to unlock his heart before thousands
and let them all come in.

Sandra Marchetti

Against Seven-Inning Doubleheaders and Starting Runners on Second Base in Extra Innings in Major League Baseball

When the infielders were tired
they just dropped their heads,
one after another, in dust
plumes along the basepaths

and big innings occurred,
stroked singles followed
each other into the dusk,
infinite batsmen moved
through their stations.

The sky turned from purple
to velvet, then a glamour
of stars. Ballcaps became
curtains, the fielders sighed
and woke up again, eyes

raised into the ready position.
The diamond itself is a galaxy,
the teams orbiting one another.
Part of the bargain is
the never-ending.

Nancy Austin

Boys and Girls of Summer

Five grandkids into T-ball, softball and baseball, we travel
a thousand miles to visit our five-year old, arrive at game time.
There he is way out in right field in full regalia
looking for bugs, butterflies, twigs, anything of interest.

My daughter elbows me to say she thinks he sees me.
He yanks off his glove, tosses it to the ground, cups hands,
shouts, *Hey everybody, look, my grandma's here,*
wrestles thumbs and forefingers into a heart, held high.

Emma's up to bat, blond curls cascading from her helmet,
big brothers standing like X's against the fence to cheer.
She cracks a ground ball short of the pitcher's mound,
the entire outfield empties to get it.

Next on deck, our little one lets his coach adjust his stance.
Swing, miss. Swing, miss. Swing, miss. A do over.
Bat finally meets ball, he beelines it towards third base,
both team's bleachers rise to direct him the other way.

Enzo's up next to prove once again there *is* crying in baseball.
His mom, baby bouncing on hip, runs interference, game ends.
Teams run the gamut of parallel lines, sweaty, extended hands,
swarm like bees to snag the best bag of chips, most colorful drink.

Donna Kelly

Summer in a Chicago Suburb not far from the Wisconsin State Line, circa 1977

It's another loss for the Cubs,
and I don't care,
because there's
Jack Brickhouse's
it's-a-swing-and-a-miss
lulling me to close my eyes,
belly-down,
on the gold-shag carpet,
my face on the rough underside
of a hand-stitched throw pillow,
only inches from the mammoth television,
that only gets clear reception
from a handful of stations—
one of which, thankfully, is WGN—

and where I can doze off to the syncopation
of those lovely long breaks
between pitches,
the warm murmur of the crowd,
like a giant hive of happy bees,
a communal hymn,
the measure of the sport,
a lackadaisical harmony,
the whir of Rick Reuschel's pitches,
right down the middle:

the contented comfort of the steady,
the belief of a known,
the becoming of a sinking strike,
a smile into the swing and a miss,
into the sleep.

Scott Lowery

Memorabilia

for Ben

sweating lunchtime beer
        Grandpa pressed white shirts
tuned in to the game

                :::

    ghost voices
Herb Carneal & Halsey Hall
       window fan   crickets

                :::

Dad could call up
        Willie Mays at Nicollet Park
now   a drive-through bank

                :::

dates & stats   fading
        even cards gone years ago
bubblegum smell   stays

                :::

    and here comes the tarp
roll & tumble   one small crew
       versus all that rain

                :::

we'd swear   carefully
       an eye on the older guys
rehearsing   all of us

                :::

                ball frozen mid-air
big as a September moon
            I still strike out

            :::

after three walks
        his eyes find me in the crowd
throw strikes   he looks down

            :::

        high fly ball
he backs up   stumbles   there
                stuck in his mitt

            :::

two Korean coins
        Chan Ho Park's rookie card
childhood   dresser drawer

            :::

        first base chalky white
recedes as I run toward it
        dreaming   even now

            :::

haiku poets
        recite & drink   grinning
box seats   third base line

Pickup Ball

For me, baseball was not about
perfectly manicured infields
megawatt sound systems
climate controlled domes
overpriced concessions
and endless pitching changes
interrupted periodically by
ten seconds of action.

Baseball was about
pickup games on an asphalt field
with painted baselines
crushed soda can bases
and a chain-link backstop.

It was about
screaming one-hoppers
caught in the palm of
my garage sale fielder's mitt
causing me to hop and flap
that stinging left hand
like it was on fire
as the batter rounded first.

It was about
pitcher's hand
ghost runners
and right field automatic outs
for lack of enough players.
For me, it was never about
multimillion dollar contracts
superstar endorsements
and twelve-dollar beers.

Jim Landwehr

It was about
bringing your own bat
sharing your glove
and four fouls is an out.

It was about
kids playing a kids' game
purely for the love of it
on a summer day.

David Jibson

On Finding a Jack Morris Baseball Card

Imagine my surprise Jack, at finding
your 1979 Topps baseball card
in a library copy of *Bullfinch's Mythology*,
as though someone thought you belonged
among the gods of Olympus
and the chivalrous knights
of King Arthur's famous round table,
not that any one of them could have matched
your 254 victories and 175 complete games
over eighteen seasons.

Of course, when I found you,
I immediately descended the stairs
to the library's reference desk
to look up what you might be worth.
The result was a disappointment,
like your 7 and 12 season with The Blue Jays.

But ask Lancelot, Borhort or Gawain
if they have four World Series rings
from four different teams,
or if Caradoc With The Shrunken Arm
would have been capable, at age thirty-six,
of pitching ten shut-out innings
in game seven against the Braves.

You're a bookmark, Jack, history lost
between the pages of a book
with a lithograph of Guinevere on its cover.
Jack Morris, Topps #251,
a $2.00 legend among myths.

Ed Werstein

Tigers #6

He was a Tiger
roaming right field
right out of high school,
youngest batting champion ever.

Instinct told him which flies
would drop into the overhang.
The others he camped under.

Line drives? He climbed the wall
preventing home runs.

At the plate, he had the sweetest swing ever
sweeter than DiMaggio's
wherever he's gone.

His hit in 1968's game five
with the Tigers facing elimination
drove in two and turned the series around.

Al Kaline, three thousand seven hits
three hundred ninety-nine home runs.

Proof that there can be more than
one battery on a baseball team.

Tim Krcmarik

The Big Hurt

Is what a pod
of portly pork belly brokers
chortling their way

to pussy and gin
calls the blue norther
tuning up a jungle

of defunct steel mills
thirty miles south
in the murder capital of the world,

while close to Chinatown
in a stadium named
for some faceless conglomerate

pedaling pussy and gin,
the north side Blues
and the south side Blacks,

all starry-eyed on coffee and speed,
lock horns
in a bi-annual bloodbath

of stale grudges and vulgarity blooms,
beer sellers stalking
an iron flock

working its powerful thirst
top of the first
on a darkling summer afternoon

Tim Krcmarik

as a pack of pimply towheads
chuck flaming toilet paper rolls
from the nosebleeds

to remind the press box they exist,
and a pigtailed kid
crushing life

at a crumbling school
you never heard of
takes a huge sip of Pepsi

and turns back to a glossy spread
about this magical giant
who can leap from half court,

whirling and windmilling
like a winged horse in white high tops,
and dunk an orange ball

so hard the universe shatters
into a billion
shimmering acts of Creation.

Greg Zeck

Boys Forever Blues

Tough loss after eighteen wins in a row
though we're still in first by two games,
sixty to go. Me and the boys been through
this how many times through the years,
chasing fly balls and fireflies all summer
long, and it still aches, watching them play
this way, winning and winning then falling
on their face at last, too few hits, too many
errors, about as bad as the day we got
the news about Tommy going down.

Back in the day, Tommy and I would hoof it
out to the real grass ballpark in the suburbs
where we lived, an erector set cantilevered over
cornfields — before he went off and played
Class A and then Class AA — where we would
take off our shirts and tan in the bleachers, flirting
with the girls in their bikinis, and one time
I remember carrying him home, because he was
barefoot as the day he was born, over the thistles
in the ditches, before he was thrown from the Harley
and his soul went down to darkest Hades.

Now the ballpark's downtown and Teflon, no
stately pleasure dome, no Kubla Khan, no dope,
no lie, and if you slam down too many Grain Belts,
six, seven bucks a cup, just in case the boys muff it,
you too might do a faceplant — on the sidewalk,
where goldenrod, chickweed, vetch, creeping
charlie, buttercup, ragwort, god knows what is
growing, in the dirty heart of the city, where nothing
by rights should grow, the way we've done nature.

Greg Zeck

So tonight just hours after we lose, I wake,
like the night I got the news, my wife beside me
sleeping peacefully, and feel the same icy horror
in my heart, the monstrous ache and emptiness
and unbelief, and a tear or two welling up also.

Tommy played two seasons in Kenosha
and Cedar Rapids and was making steady
progress and believed in two more years
he'd be in the bigs, shagging flies under azure
skies and hitting wicked liners like only he could,
when the Harley hit a patch of oil in the road
and flipped three or four times, and Tommy,
who was barefoot once again like the boys
of summer, boys forever, and without a helmet
or a saving grace at this point to his name, went
flying over the handlebars and cracked his skull
open like a bloody egg.

So this is a game, I say, a game we love, win or
lose, played under filthy Teflon or on green grass.
If you don't wanna lose, don't play, I say, and if you
win don't take it too much to heart 'cause the hurt
is real when it comes, and it will come, 'cause we're
just passing through, every damned last mother's
son one and all, smiling into the sunshine, closing
our eyes on the gloom, and isn't it about time
for one more goddamn Grain Belt after all? *Prosit*!

Peter M. Gordon

I Want to Be Married at Home Plate

My bride in a frilly white dress spilling over the
white rectangle marking
the left hand batter's box

She twists her spikes into sugary dirt digging in at
the back of the box peering
over her shoulder and through the veil at

Lefty, the minister, toeing the pitcher's rubber
Day so dazzling we wear long brim caps
Bride slowly swings her bat back and forth

I race in from third in my morning coat
Execute a perfect hook slide around the catcher
shower brown clay all over her dress

She pulls me to stand by her side
We brush each other off, grab bats
crouch in our boxes, stare down Lefty.

Who lobs in a softball: "do you promise to
cleave to one another,
forsaking all others?"

We knock it out of the park. Start life
together dirty sliding home just
under the tag.

Mary McKSchmidt

Setting the Record Straight

For Harry Stapler, former publisher of the East Lansing Towne Courier

What you may not know about Billy Martin
is that in January of 1972, the same year
he took the Detroit Tigers to their first

American League East Championship,
he met a young woman sports editor
on a Tiger preseason press tour.

It was the first time a woman
had crossed the threshold into a room
of Tigers mingling with the press and she

was greeted with a silence so deafening
for decades she lived in the shadow
of that nightmare. It would not fade.

What you may not know about Billy Martin
is that unlike others in the room that night,
he did not hit on her. Maybe somehow he knew

that she, like he, had a tough job. Perhaps
he saw her at the door taking a deep breath,
squaring her shoulders before stepping into the ring.

Perhaps it touched in him the sense of chivalry seeded
by the mother and grandmother who raised him
after his father deserted them. This player-turned-manager,

renowned for throwing punches, kicking dust
and waging war with his own front office, decided
to share with the tenacious woman his untold backstory.

Mary McKSchmidt

She was twenty, too young, too naïve to know
that what's told to the press is on the record,
unless it's not. Billy Martin never said it was not.

Fearing his candid details too personal to publish,
she decided not to write the article. Only later,
when Billy Martin repeated his story

to a male reporter and it appeared in *Sports Illustrated*,
did she realize he had been opening a door for her
into the major league of sports reporting.

What you may not know about Billy Martin
is that on learning she'd never been to Tiger Stadium,
he invited her to a game, suggested she join the team

in the dugout for pre-game batting practice.
When she arrived that mid-August afternoon,
the Tigers, after riding high in July, were in a slump

so long and ugly some were calling it fatal.
What you may not know about Billy Martin
is that while the players were like brothers to him—

he talked with them, believed in them, fought for them—
there was nothing he could do to get them through a slump
but plan more practices, say little, support their superstitions.

> *If I play well one night, I'll wear the same socks the next.
> I'm wearing too many clean socks.*
>   Ike Brown, pinch hitter, infielder

Mary McKSchmidt

It's hard to correct things under pressure so I sing, entertain the team with my great wit, and I do a lot of praying.
    Norm Cash, first baseman

I want a win so badly, I'm swinging at bad pitches.
    Ed Brinkman, shortstop

I'm not superstitious but the rosin bag is always in the exact same spot just right of the pitcher's mound.
    Joe Coleman, pitcher

I used to touch 3rd base on my way out to centerfield, but I kept tripping over the bag so I quit.
    Mickey Stanley, centerfielder

What you may not know about Billy Martin
is that when the woman in the dugout suggested
he sign for her a practice ball to bring them luck,

he borrowed her pen, signed the ball, then
tossed both ball and pen to the players nearby.
The remainder of that championship year

is Tiger history. Ask any fan.

Jocelyn Boor

Baseball for Girls

My grandpa took me to baseball games
When I was three years old.
The Rockford Peaches.
Instead of popcorn
I wanted to play.

NO, said Mom and grandma
Girls don't do that
So they gave me dolls.

But in 7th grade we girls played softball
While the boys played baseball.
We protested.
And one day the boys' team played us.
Baseball rules.
In the outfield, I ran to catch
A speeding zinger.
Dropped my mitt.
Caught the ball, barehanded.
We won!
And I broke my middle finger.
Haven't played since.
But I watch and swear well.

Susan Haifleigh

McGill Drive

Summer was our sabbatical, a winner over textbooks
and rolling out of bed at 5:30 a.m. to catch the bus,
summer was freedom, ushering in fresh syncopated rhythms.

We passed boredom back and forth,
counting down the hazy days by carving lines
with worn red pocketknives into the trunk
of the big tree on the corner, our only clock.

We swam in the pond, biked the looped street,
napped in the shady meadow, built forts
in the strongest tree, lifting the rope ladders
up and inside, keeping the younger kids out.

Pride seeped across the neighbor's yards,
freshly mowed and edged, sprinklers whooshing
away the heat of burning pavement.
Houses sat clustered together, leaning in
and gossiping among themselves.

At least twice every season we would abandon
the neighborhood ball game and run screaming
behind a battered old truck dispensing toxic
mosquito-killing fog, it never occurred to us,
or our parents, that this might not be a good idea.

Like Tom Sawyer, we yearned for the big world, safe in our little one.
Trips to McDonald's constituted the entirety of the bigger world.
If we begged and pleaded my sister would acquiesce,
an excuse to lord her teen power over us, while her learner's permit
barely allowed her to back down the driveway.

Susan Haifleigh

Now the back stop is gone, the ballfield un-mowed,
we have dispersed like dandelion seeds,
planted and fully grown in every place imaginable.
What I wouldn't give to have just one of them here,
to welcome boredom, passing it back and forth between us.

Jeffrey Johannes

Jimmy

I almost expected a vapor trail
as the ball went up, up, up
and lingered in afternoon light

before descending beyond
the outfield fence where we stood
with mitts in hand after a long day

sweating in the canning factory,
each crack of Jimmy's bat
speaking the language of summer.

How I'd love to live again the joy
of spotting that dot of white
against blue sky, my heart

pounding when a ball smacked
into my glove from the powerhouse
bat of a future Wisconsin hero soon

to be known as Gumby to teammates
as they played their way to the
American League Championship.

Ohtani Imayo

Shohei stands in *no kamae*, samurai in cleats:
his bat, like a blade held high. He straddles the plate
with a presence that commands; his swing follows through,
then cleaves the air with finesse—to lay waste with grace.

Tom Conlan

Baseball Intervenes

in a boy's life
like a freight train running down the tracks
where we stuck pennies in iron gaps
hid in the bushes while steel wheels
flattened coins into souvenirs

A small plane crashed into a wheat field
across the railroad bridge over a clear stream
where trout surely roamed
We got to the broken plane before anyone else
except the pilot, who safely walked away

Baseball or fishing—had to make a choice
what with so many other important tasks
to while away our sunny, summer afternoons

Evenings reserved for organized Little League games
after the coaches got out of work
Never as much fun as the pickup matches
down by the creek—where in our minds
Maris and Mantle battled away against Kaline, Colavito, and Cash

Played until someone hit a homer into the woods
and after a half-hearted search
we lost the last ragged, taped-up ball.

Joe Carey

Baseball and My Dad

Watching baseball with my dad
makes time stop and take
a breather,
like a seventh-inning stretch.
We're not moving, just seated still,
next to one another,
two people on a planet spinning
through space,
taking time to watch a game
with a ball and bat and
advertisements all around as
far as the eye can see.
Could anything be better
than sipping a lemonade next
to him & seeing the gloriously
striped green field as one?

Bruce Dethlefsen

Sixty-one

monday I crossed off cowboy
tuesday fireman
wednesday president
thursday I couldn't find the list
friday my own fishing show
saturday catching for the Cardinals
sunday I took a nap
sorry
I had to
the moons flew by too soon

Tom Erickson

Baseball

"Middle age is the enemy of art." Orson Welles

The enemy of my writing is baseball. In my middle age, I can watch baseball on TV all day long as I will myself to some dangerous edge of absorption.

Why are some lefthanders harder on right-handers than lefthanders? It's mind-boggling. Like a koan from Kung Fu. Tell me what is Buddha and then tell me why this pitcher's reverse splits defy all logic.

How come fastballs are on average three mph faster than ten years ago? The easy answer is PEDs but that doesn't make sense because baseball is clean now, right little naïve Weedhopper?

Why is the foul pole fair?

When I do go to games I always keep score. I didn't know why until I read the small type on the program: "Your scorecard will serve as a written memento and historical record of the game." So there.

It's better to stay home, to run home, to go home than go to the park because on TV you can watch the catcher give the signs to the pitcher. Give me a beer, let me sit in my blue chair with the windows open and, as night falls, anticipate the next pitch. The whole game could pivot on the next ten seconds 250 times a game. Man oh man oh man...

My grandfather lived by himself in a trailer at the end of a road in a little town where he played centerfield in his youth. At the end of his life, he was almost blind so he would sit right in front of the TV, lean in on his cane, and peer at the Tigers game. The closer he got to the screen, the easier it was to get lost in the rhythms of the game; the easier it was, in his old age, to let the imponderable be.

Sandra Marchetti

Friday, 1:20

If you shut
your eyes

you'll forget
where you are

and hear
the nature

of real things.
From your seat

the long, low
call of the hot

dog vendor is
a mourning dove

singing to
those he loves.

Ode to Baseball

You shine through the bright summer season,
displayed in that space both emerald and diamond,
your history recorded in sagas of rookie seasons
and career years, encoded in tables of RBI and ERA,
demanding the impossible and conferring greatness
upon those who fail only two-thirds of the time.

No other game is so unhurried in ebb and flow,
opening up time for talk, room for words,
the pop fly and the sky ball,
the line drive and the frozen rope,
the untouchable seeing-eye single,
and the dying quail, faltering back to earth.

The batter in his box fears the high and the hard,
the chin music, waits for the curve that hangs,
the breaking ball that does not break,
hopes to deliver the grand slam,
the matchless grandeur of the gesture
and the brute force of the blow.

Through the long quest of the season,
you record our failures in errors and in balks,
grant redemption with the sacrifice and the steal,
promise that relief will come when it is needed most,
and preserve until the last batter of this timeless game
our humble hope, to make it safely home.

Acknowledgements

"Pitchers and Catchers" by Patrick Walsh first appeared in *Spitball*.

"Spring: A Catechism" by Amy Miller first appeared in *Borderlands: Texas Poetry Review*

"Town Ball" by Vince Wixom first appeared in *Spitball*

"Looking Out This Window Thinking of Ernie Banks and William Carlos Williams" by Kevin Miller first appeared in *Spring Meditation*

"Extending Her Contract" by Milton Jordan first appeared in *Texas Poetry Assignment*

"At the Mazeroski Wall PNC Bank Park, Pittsburgh, PA" and " Lou Gehrig Day Yankee Stadium, July 4, 1939" by Edwin Romond first appeared in *Home Team: Poems About Baseball*

"Johnny Callison" by Joseph Chelios first appeared in *Spitball*

"Bat Day at the Met" and "Pickup Ball" by Jim Landwehr first appeared in *Tea in the Pacific Northwest*

"Baseball" by Mark Hammerschick first appeared in *East on Central*

"Three Baseball Haiku" by Sylvia Forges-Ryan first appeared in *Baseball Haiku*

"108 (2016 World Series)" by Timothy Tocher first appeared in *Spitball*

"Caught in the Web" by Jack Ridl first appeared in *Aethlon*

"Against Seven Inning Double Headers" by Sandra Marchetti first appeared in *Blackbird*, and her poem "Friday, 1:20" first appeared in *TAB*

"Baseball" by Tom Erickson appeared in *The Pacific Review*

About the Poets

Nancy Austin serves as the Northwest Region VP of the Wisconsin Fellowship of Poets, has been published in various journals, and has four poetry collections. Find her at nancyaustinauthor.com.

Julián David Bañuelos is a Chicano poet and translator from Texas whose work appears in several literary journals. He teaches in New York City.

Georgi Bargamian writes poetry and prose about loss, longing, identity and heritage. She lives in Ann Arbor, Michigan.

Jocelyn Boor, Grafton, Wisconsin, retired teacher who continues to write and learn and has published in the annual Wisconsin Poets Calendar while keeping one ear attuned to sports.

Dwayne Brenna has been a school bus driver, a baseball poet, a Doctor of Philosophy, a car wash attendant, a Shakespearean actor, and a university professor. He lives and writes in Saskatoon.

Paul Buchheit is an author of books, poems, and progressive essays. His most recent book is *365 Sonnets: Celebrating Each Day with a "Little Song,"* published in May, 2025.

Maggie Capettini is an artist-turned-poet who grew up in a Cubs family in Chicago's western suburbs. She married into a White Sox family. This is her first publication.

Joseph Kuhn Carey's three books of poetry are: *Sunrise over South Africa* (Kelsay Books, 2025), *Black Forest Dreams* (Kelsay Books, 2021) and *Postcards from Poland* (Chicago Poetry Press, 2014). www.josephkuhncareycreativeworks.com

Patricia Carragon hosts Brownstone Poets and is the editor-in-chief of its annual anthology. She edits *Sense & Sensibility Haiku Journal*. Human Error Publishing accepted her poetry manuscript, *Stranger on the Shore*.

Joseph Chelius, a devoted Phillies fan, is the author of two collections of poems with WordTech Communications. His new collection, *Playing Fields*, was published by Kelsay Books in 2025.

Robert Chicoine fifteen years ago traded in morning workout for poetry. The mind much clearer now, if the body less in shape. Fifty syllables are easier than five sit-ups!

Jan Chronister lives in Maple, Wisconsin, and Albany, Georgia. She played sandlot baseball as a kid. She now devotes her time to gardening and poetry.

Dennis Collier of Madison, WI, a retired fiscal policy analyst and former newspaper editor, returned after decades away from poetry when taking a course on the Psalms.

Tom Conlan lives in the highlands of Northern Michigan. He has published three full-length books and appears in numerous literary journals. Find his new visual poetry collection – *Secret Conversations* online at www.thomasfordconlan.com

Bill Cushing, originally from New York, has lived in numerous states, the Virgin Islands, Puerto Rico, and now Los Angeles. Bill has published five poetry collections; his latest is *The Beast Inside*.

Sharon Daly left the land of the Pittsburgh Pirates in childhood for Midwest fields and now calls Wisconsin home, on deck for inspiration to strike.

David Dephy is an award-winning American poet, the founder of Poetry Orchestra. He serves as the Poet-in-Residence for Brownstone Poets for 2024-2025. He lives and works in New York City.

Bruce Dethlefsen grew up playing catcher in the Kansas City youth baseball program. A fan of the hapless Athletics in the 1950's, Bruce became Wisconsin Poet Laureate (2011-2012).

Susan Firer is a past Milwaukee Poet Laureate and recipient of a NEA Fellowship. Her poems have appeared in many publications, including *The New Yorker*, *Best American Poetry*, *Ms Magazine* and others.

Sylvia Forges-Ryan edited Frogpond, the journal of the Haiku Society of America, from 1991 through 1993. Author of three acclaimed poetry books, her haiku have received numerous international prizes and awards.

Peter M. Gordon is an award-winning poet with over 188 poems published in various journals, along with three collections available on amazon.com. He teaches in Full Sail University's FPMFA program.

Barbara Anna Gaiardoni is among the winners of the 7th Basho - an international haiku competition. Her Japanese-style poetry has been published in 250 international magazines and translated into 12 languages. http://barbaragaiardoni.altervista.org/blog/haikuco-2-2/

Susan Haifleigh is an architect by training, poet by design. Publications: *Story Medicine, Stafford Challenge Anthology, Beyond Words, Peninsula Poets, Fahmidan, Women Raise Our Voices.* She lives near the Detroit Tigers home field!

Mark Hammerschick writes poetry and fiction. He holds a BA in English from the University of Illinois at Champaign-Urbana and a BS and MBA.

Alan Harris is Vice-President and proud manager of the UAW Local 2256 Softball Team. His poetry graces the concrete sidewalk at the entrance of Lansing, Michigan's minor league baseball stadium.

Ronnie Hess grew up nearsighted in New York and never could throw straight. She is a Mets fan and lives in Madison.

Mandi Butterfield Isaacson co-ran a monthly poetry reading in Oshkosh on Tuesday evenings, until the COVID era. She's had numerous original poems published in the annual *Wisconsin Poets' Calendar*.

David Jibson is the editor of *3rd Wednesday Magazine*. He's retired from a long career in Social Work, most recently with a hospice agency.

Jeffrey Johannes, Port Edwards, WI, has a new chapbook *Coffee Quiet* from Kelsay Books. He has co-edited the WFOP Calendar and Bramble, and won the Hal Prize.

Milton Jordan participates in the online community Texas Poetry Assignment where he first shared the poem "Extending Her Contract." His poetry has appeared in print and online journals.

Dan Kaufman lives near Jacksonville, Oregon. His poetry has appeared in print and online. Dan facilitates a monthly poetry open mic at the Talent Library.

Donna Kathryn Kelly [@donnakathrynkelly.com] is the author of *The Cheney Manning Series*, a trilogy of suspense novels about an Illinois public defender turned amateur sleuth who investigates homicide cases.

Tim Krcmarik is a Truck 3 Captain with the Austin Fire Department. He has eighteen years on the job, and lives in Austin, Texas with his wife and son.

Jim Landwehr has six books of poetry and four full-length memoirs. He is poet laureate emeritus for the Village of Wales, Wisconsin and lives in Waukesha, Wisconsin.

Scott Lowery grew up in Minneapolis and now lives in Milwaukee near his grandchildren. Find his two chapbooks, other publications, and workshops with young writers at www.scottlowery.org.

Sandra Marchetti won the 2023 Twin Bill Book Prize for Best Baseball Poetry Book. She's authored three poetry collections: *DIORAMA* (SFASUP, 2025); *Aisle 228* (SFASUP, 2023); and *Confluence* (Sundress, 2015).

Mary McKSchmidt's life has zigzagged from newspapers to corporations to advocating for the Great Lakes and seniors. She writes poetry to reveal and weave the jagged threads that are her.

Amy Miller's latest books are *Astronauts*, a finalist for the Oregon Book Award, and *The Trouble with New England Girls*. She lives in southern Oregon.

Kevin Miller's collection, *Spring Meditation*, was published by MoonPath Press, 2022. His collection, *Vanish*, received the Wandering Aengus Press Publication Award in 2019. He lives in Tacoma, Washington.

Darrell Petska is a retired university engineering editor and three-time Pushcart Prize nominee. See conservancies.wordpress.com for his published poetry and fiction. He lives near Madison, Wisconsin.

Jack Ridl was named Michigan's Professor of the year by the Carnegie Foundation. More than 100 of his students are published authors. A former shortstop, Jack has published eight collections.

James P. Roberts has baseball in his blood, spending his childhood living behind the local minor league stadium in Waterloo, Iowa. He now lives in Madison, Wisconsin.

Edwin Romond's most recent book is *Man at the Railing* (NYQ Books,) winner of the 2022 Laura Boss Narrative Poetry Award. He lives in Wind Gap, PA.

Margaret R. Sáraco has always been a Mets fan and poet. Margaret published two poetry books: *If There Is No Wind* and *Even the Dog Was Quiet* (Human Error Publishing.)

Sara Sarna is a poet, actor, and avid hiker. She enjoys membership in Wisconsin Fellowship of Poets, Wisconsin Writers Association, Write On, Door County and Hartford Avenue Poets.

Virginia Small grew up on a farm in New Berlin, Wisconsin. She has written and published poetry since her teens and continues to publish articles about environmental and civic issues.

Mark Tardi is a writer and translator originally from Chicago on faculty at the University of Łódź. His newest book is *Recapitulation in the Wrong Key* (BlazeVOX, 2025).

Timothy Tocher is the author of five sports-themed books for middle grade and teen readers. He has published dozens of short stories, poems, and nonfiction articles for all ages.

Pepper Trail's poems have appeared in *Atlanta Review*, *Rattle*, *Catamaran*, and elsewhere. His collection, *Cascade-Siskiyou: Poems* was a finalist for the Oregon Book Award. He lives in Ashland, OR.

Peggy Trojan lives in Brule, Wisconsin and has published two full-length poetry collections and eight chapbooks. Her books are available on Amazon.

Patrick Walsh's poems have appeared in *Barrow Street*, *Evergreen Review*, *Hudson Review*, *Malahat Review*, *Poetry New Zealand*, *Vallum*, the first issue of *THE SHOp*, and *War, Literature & the Arts*.

Mario "The Poet" Willis, spoken word artist and Milwaukee native, has been featured throughout the Midwest. He is a writing guide and performance coach. A two-time member of Milwaukee's National Poetry Slam Team, Mario served as the Milwaukee Public Library Poet Laureate (2022-2024).

Vince Wixon (Ashland, OR)—a Giants fan since 1954—is the author of three books of poetry, most recently *Laying By* (Flowstone), and co-editor of four books by William Stafford.

Greg Zeck, a Minnesota native, has published poetry in the little magazines and in three collections of his own (available at Amazon). For more info, see www.youngzeck.com.

Mark Zimmermann's "Powell" will appear in his forthcoming poetry book *Bomb Threats* from Pebblebrook Press. He lives in Milwaukee with his wife Carole and cat Katinka.

About the Editors

Tom Erickson grew up in Kohler, Wisconsin, where he played a lot of baseball. He is an attorney in Milwaukee and is a member of the Hartford Avenue Poets. He is also the author of five poetry books including *The Lawyer Who Died in the Courthouse Bathroom* (Parallel Press, the University of Wisconsin Libraries, 2013) and *Cutting the Dusk in Half* (Bent Paddle Press, 2022) which each received awards. He is a devout fan of the Milwaukee Brewers and knows there is always next year.

Ed Werstein is a fan of both the Detroit Tigers and the Milwaukee Brewers, and hopes they will face off in the World Series some day. He is a member of the Wisconsin Fellowship of Poets and the Hartford Avenue Poets. He published his first poem at the age of sixty. Since then he has placed over 200 poems in various journals, and has published four volumes of poetry which can be found on his website: edwerstein.com. In 2018 he won the Council for Wisconsin Writers Lorine Niedecker Award, judged by Nickole Brown.

www.ingramcontent.com/pod-product-compliance
Lightning Source LLC
Chambersburg PA
CBHW030529080526
44586CB00011B/381